house beautiful

WINDOWS

house beautiful

WINDOWS

The Editors of House Beautiful Magazine

Louis Oliver Gropp, Editor in Chief ⊞ Margaret Kennedy, Editor

Text by Sally Clark

HEARST BOOKS
NEW YORK

It is the policy of William Morrow and Company, Inc., and its imprints and affiliates, recognizing the importance of preserving what has been written, to print the books we publish on acid-free paper, and we exert our best efforts to that end.

Library of Congress Cataloging-in-Publication Data

Clark, Sally.
House beautiful windows / the editors of House Beautiful magazine : text by Sally Clark.
p. cm. — (Great style series)
ISBN 0-688-14473-X
1. Drapery in interior decoration. 2. Window shades. 3. Blinds.
I. House beautiful. II. Title. III. Series.
NK2115.5.D73C53 1997
747'.5—dc20 96-33461
CIP

Printed in Italy
First Edition
1 2 3 4 5 6 7 8 9 10

Edited by Laurie Orseck ⊞ Designed by Pat Tan
Produced by Smallwood & Stewart, Inc., New York

contents

FOREWORD

Overlooking the Hudson River and Riverside Park from our Manhattan apartment, and sitting in the midst of a wooded acre at our house in the country, my own window treatments are of the most minimal variety. I always favor a less-is-more approach to design and decoration; as a result, you'll find many window treatments in this book to be of striking simplicity. But we at *House Beautiful* enjoy interiors that are rich and dense and full of the delights of more abundant decorating as well, so you will also find windows that appear to be dressed for a ball, or at least a party, in the pages that follow. That has historically been our philosophy of decorating: a wealth of choices to let readers find and choose the style that best suits their personal taste and circumstances.

Whether you want your windows to star or play a supporting role, you will find ideas for almost any type of decoration. And whether your windows are architectural gems that frame beautiful views or awkward design problems with no view at all, this book was created to help you make the most of what you have. As the writer of *Windows*, the latest in *House Beautiful*'s Great Style series, suggests, windows can and often do determine the character of a room. You will see what she means, and what we intended, when you study the many examples in the chapters ahead. Enjoy.

Louis Oliver Gropp
EDITOR IN CHIEF

INTRODUCTION

Window decorations are the grand finishing touch in a room. More than most other components of design, they are charged with multiple roles embracing beauty and function. On the practical side, they control light and ventilation and provide the sheltering luxury of privacy. Visually, they are the great aesthetic unifiers, the major elements that bring the walls and windows together in decorative harmony and ensure that they blend with the style of the room.

Such a vast array of styles exists that it is possible to create any number of looks and moods with a mere flip of a valance. Flowing curtains soften a room. But replace them with mahogany venetian blinds and the room takes on a tailored, architectural demeanor. Sometimes, too, a window, and the view it frames, are so beautiful in their own right that no window dressing at all is the best choice.

House Beautiful Windows offers designs in every conceivable style and proves that memorable treatments can be achieved at every budget level: easily stitched curtains wittily trimmed with loopy ties and dressmaker confections run up from sheets, as well as a host of creations painted, crafted, and sewn to order. Most of the rooms in the pages that follow were created by design professionals, and the various ways they have elected to decorate the windows ~ dressing them up or down, embellishing them richly or leaving them totally bare ~ provide an exciting starting point for planning window designs for every room.

The book's photographs beautifully illustrate such unique designs as painted trompe l'oeil swags, witty trimmed valances inspired by jesters' caps, curtain jewels borrowed from nature ~ a twiggy branch used as a curtain rod, trim concocted from seashells ~ and serve as a rich international portfolio of styles, from a Caribbean condominium with exotic carved Indian screens to a Milanese villa in which simple cotton shades underscore the owner's taste for spare, contemporary decor. By studying the photographs and finding ideas to borrow, rework, and improve upon, you will be taking the first step in creating designs that bring radiant style to every window of your home.

part one

THROUGH THE LOOKING GLASS

Windows are the eyes of a house, and perhaps it is true that in them can be discerned its character and very soul. A grandly arched Palladian window, a small colonial saltbox window, a crystalline sweep of glass ~ the shape and proportion of each reflect the style of the house they adorn. From the inside, windows are vitally tied to the architecture, too. High ceilings, for example, are an open invitation to create rich swags, fancy pelmets, or a lush cascade of richly striped fabric, as French designer Denis Colomb did in the room pictured on the opposite page. But done-up windows can suffocate a room that has small dimensions or low ceilings. "Sometimes the best thing to do with a window is nothing at all," suggested legendary designer Billy Baldwin, underscoring the appeal of the undressed window. Elsie de Wolfe, America's first decorator, had a different set of requirements: curtains for privacy at night, and, by day, uncluttered panes filled with sunshine and appealing views. The art of window decoration certainly has its practical side in controlling light and affording privacy, but a beautiful window, de Wolfe was fond of saying, should be "such a gay, animate thing."

style-setters

Window decorations play many roles in the drama called style, from stars to supporting players. Billy Baldwin was a master of understatement when it came to their treatment. For tailored and casual rooms, he often used wooden shutters that made the windows fade into the general architecture of the space. For formal settings, he liked flowing curtains that framed the windows, and he designed them with utter simplicity, usually dispensing with valances and trim. If the curtains were solid-colored ~ and they often were in Baldwin's rooms ~ the fabric was usually the same tone as the walls or one that blended discreetly with them. As a result, the walls and windows always read as a harmonious whole, a serene background to show off the furniture, antiques, and art.

Sister Parish, by contrast, liked bold windows. She often achieved a dramatic effect by using contrast with flair, selecting for the curtains a print or color of fabric that appeared nowhere else in the room. Bold valances also made her windows showy and dramatic. Even when the curtains were a neutral cream color, she added deep valances with tucks and rich fringe that made the whole window stand out importantly.

For an elegant drawing room, designer Mario Buatta created exquisite festoons of striped silk taffeta lined with silk tattersall. Thick green cord and a quartet of plump bow-style pinwheel rosettes of the same material accentuate the curve of the curtain cornice. This style, widely used in eighteenth-century Europe, "is a wonderful way to get as much light and view into the room as possible," says Buatta. The curtain completely covers the window when lowered.

In general, in a room with good antique furniture and art, solid colors are often the best choice, since printed fabrics might overpower the artwork. However, a very bold print at the window can make up for the absence of art, which is worth considering for those just starting to decorate their home. A brilliant color at the windows will also "fill up" the walls. Yellow, orange, coral, soft red, and cyclamen pink are all good choices, especially if the room faces north or has little natural light.

Sometimes it is so easy to take window treatments for granted as nothing more than sun shields and guardians of privacy that their powers of transformation are overlooked. A decorator who had arranged for her own living room curtains to be sent out for cleaning while she was away on vacation was stunned at the sight of bare walls and windows when she returned. What she saw was an unremarkable, boxy apartment space, not the cheerful and warm English-country-style room she had loved. She had grown so accustomed to the chintz draperies and pretty swagged valances that she had quite forgotten the majestic difference they made in the room ~ until they were gone.

In a stroke of delicious irony, brown striped silk that reads like the mahogany slats of old-fashioned wooden venetian blinds ties together the window wall of a smartly casual Manhattan living room designed by Joseph Lembo and Laura Bohn. The broad Regency stripes are wide enough to tame the great stretch of French windows, and the repeated pattern introduces a strong texture that warms up the pistachio walls. In keeping with the easy-going chic decor of the room, the curtains are hung on a hospital track fixture and loosely caught back with a simple thick rope.

Exuberantly swagged and fringed curtains emphasize the graceful proportions of the drawing room in decorator Jane Churchill's London town house without blocking out daylight (below). The fully gathered curtain panels, hung beyond the window frames and overlapping on the walls, act as a sumptuous frame for the giant sash windows. Their pale blue color and lavish gathers soften the entire room.

In contrast to the silky fine fabric of Churchill's curtains, designer Richard Keith Langham chose rough-woven hopsacking for the living room of a weekend home in Virginia (opposite). The casual fabric reinforces the house's relaxed atmosphere, while the curtains' stately silhouette and overscale fringe-trimmed swags underscore the height of the windows.

CLASSIC ROSES

Dressing a window in an unexpected style energizes a room. In a dining room filled with beautifully crafted reproduction pieces inspired by early-nineteenth-century Russian antiques (opposite), curtains of opulent silk would be the conventional choice. The sheer flutter of organdy trimmed with scarlet grosgrain ribbon comes as a surprise, a refreshing companion to the lavishly gilded exotic woods.

Sophistication reigns in the dining room of designer Albert Hadley's Connecticut weekend house (above). The walls are a chic glossy brown and the English Regency chairs are exquisitely carved ~ hardly the usual setting for a cotton café curtain of utter simplicity. The style should deceive no one, however; the curtain's carefully executed soft pleats and the substantial way it hangs are marks of expert workroom craftsmanship.

The spit-and-polished uniforms of a brass band might have inspired the smartly tailored Manhattan apartment of designer T. Keller Donovan. He outfitted an awkward off-center window with white venetian blinds, then flanked it with white screens; their red borders are as spiffy as the banding on a drum major's trousers.

balancing acts

Window decorations are a marvelous means of bringing harmony and balance to a room. They can underscore the inherent beauty of windows with good lines or, with a few sleight-of-hand maneuvers, improve the look of those that are not quite perfect. Playing with the width and length of curtains or shades, adding a deep valance, or hanging the whole treatment higher or wider can alter the proportions of a window, the majesty of a room, the warmth of a house.

The most obvious "rule" ~ that the scale of a successful window decoration should always be in harmony with the walls and windows of the room ~ is unfortunately not always followed. Too often, a curtain panel is too short, or stock-size louvered wooden shutters are too small. Curtains that are too narrow are a common problem, especially when trying to fit standard sizes available at retail to the nonstandard windows of many rooms. It is important, too, that all aspects of a window treatment ~ the length and width of panels, the depth of a valance, the size of the rod, holdbacks, and any other hardware ~ are in proportion as well. A big window deserves generous embellishments; undersize hardware and flimsy rods will automatically underplay its inherent drama and grandness.

Scale also plays a crucial role in the choice of fabrics with pattern or print. Tiny, dainty prints are charming on a small window, but they will be completely lost on a large one. By the same token, a dynamic print may totally overwhelm a small or even a medium-size window. And the width of a stripe or the grid of a plaid should be selected with the window's overall proportions in mind.

How a patterned fabric will appear when it is sewn is often overlooked. If the treatment is to sit flat, as it does with a fabric shade, the complete pattern will be on view; if the patterned fabric is gathered or shirred into a curtain panel, the design will appear compressed when the curtain is hung. Some large-scale prints that look beautiful when they are flat will be too "busy" if they are made into gathered curtains. As a test before purchasing, try bunching together a generous section of fabric in the hand to discover if it holds its appeal. Also check the repeat of the pattern ~ how wide the complete pattern is. It is definitely worth purchasing a yard or two to try at home before making an investment, especially an expensive one. Some stores even loan out bolts of fabric for overnight tryouts.

Bypassing neutral and unobtrusive fabric, Christian Badin designed a large-scale pattern in silk especially for the curtains in Barbara Wirth's Paris drawing room. The yellow is a perfect shade to offset the city's gray light and makes every day deceivingly sunny. The curtains fall straight to the floor from a rod attached to the cornice, thus underscoring the room's double-height ceiling.

The buttery color-washed walls and marble-like painted floors of a living room designed by Ned Marshall were inspired by Italian villas he had visited; the curtains took their cue from the antic liveliness of a fool's cap, complete with bells. The valances crowning the sash windows (above and right) are made from striped cotton-linen fabric ornamented with small wooden bells. In a variation on that design, the draperies on the large window (right) are embellished with a heading of folded-over points cut from gold silk-and-cotton faille. The design has the amusing effect of a collar on a jester's costume.

THE VILLAS OF TUSCANY

In the living room of a house in Washington, D.C. (opposite), designer Mary Douglas Drysdale avoided the typical neutral background art collectors often choose. Instead she glazed the walls brilliant yellow and put a mandarin-orange material ~ a synthetic that looks like silk taffeta ~ on the windows. In this sunny room, the orange color provides perpetual radiance. In the dining room (above), also filled with good contemporary art, Drysdale hung a yellow and white striped balloon shade. When she couldn't find a fabric with stripes wide enough to carry off the effect she envisioned, she had her workroom create it by sewing together strips of yellow and white cotton chintz. The resulting stripes are bold enough to stand up to the large floor-to-ceiling window.

Elegant white curtains are a classic choice to bring out the harmonious proportions of the European-style drawing room. In antiques dealer Louis Bofferding's living room, sunlight shines through the richly gathered curtains. From a rod secured at cornice level, the snowy draperies spill to the floor like a bridal gown and draw attention to the luxurious height of the room's French doors.

rooms with a view

The poet Robert Frost wrote that good fences make good neighbors. The same can be said of window coverings. Windows that open onto a beautiful view are priceless, but curtains and shades are equally invaluable for privacy, especially where the windows of neighboring houses and apartments look into one another, and in personal spaces such as bedrooms, bathrooms, and dressing rooms. For these rooms, the answer might be a double treatment: matchstick blinds close to the window to filter the light by day and full-length curtains that can be pulled together at night for added privacy.

Window coverings also play an important role in controlling light. In rooms with large windows, they provide a comfort shield against the sun's glare and heat. Often the best choices for rooms that face into the sun are wooden venetian blinds, vertical blinds, or mini blinds with narrow slats of plastic or aluminum featuring cords, wands, or other mechanisms that allow the light to be finely calibrated. A growing concern about the harmful effects of ultraviolet rays has given rise to a variety of solar screening materials, including a scrimlike plastic mesh that works well for large window walls in contemporary settings.

For many people, being able to draw a curtain at night provides a measure of psychological comfort as well as an aesthetic way of blocking out the blackness that fills a window after sundown. Its more practical function is to block out the glare of streetlamps and car lights, which can even plague houses in the country that seem perfectly situated by day. The glow of the full moon and the shimmering light of dawn may be the stuff of poetry, but to the light-sensitive sleeper they are the ruin of sound slumber. Equipping bedroom windows with double treatments such as heavy shades and curtains with thick linings usually solves the problem. Some designers even suggest using theatrical blackout cloth as the ultimate curtain lining.

Window dressings ~ especially those made of soft fabric ~ can also act as an insulation against noise, muffling street sounds outside as well as absorbing noise in the room itself. Installing curtains is the quickest way to take the echoes out of a new house, even if there is little furniture in it.

In a New York City apartment overlooking Central Park, custom-tailored roll-down shades ensure privacy. The simple treatment chosen by designer Vicente Wolf also keeps the room from getting too formal for the casual young family who lives there.

With its spectacular views, a Manhattan apartment (left and opposite) is "meant to be like an observation tower," says Lee Mindel. His architecture firm transformed the once cookie-cutter apartment into flowing white-on-white spaces where streams of sunlight tinge the rooms shades of gold and rose depending on the time of day. As a shield against ultra-violet rays, the architects installed shades made of sun-filtering plastic mesh at every window. Lowered, the shades resemble scrims.

OTTO WAGNER
Inigo Jones

White linen Roman shades make the windows "feel bigger and cleaner," says the owner of this weekend country house. Curtains over the room's seven windows "would have looked too fabric-y," she explains. She opted instead for a more architectural solution and chose the chalk-white linen to meld with the white woodwork. Cut amply to cover the side moldings, the shades are weighted at the bottom with a rod that forces them to hang in a tailored way. Plastic stays keep the big linen folds neatly in place when the shades are raised.

Flowing draperies layered over matchstick blinds give designer Craig Raywood's study a very traditional appearance, offering no hint that the room is on the thirtieth floor of a new luxury apartment building in New York City. The ultimate splurge is barely visible: The curtain fabric is lined with yellow cashmere.

This two-tier treatment marries fully gathered damask curtains with functional venetian blinds. Hanging the curtains from poles set several inches above the window molding and letting the damask panels tumble to the floor gives the ordinary double-hung sash windows a more distinguished look.

A variety of curtain fabrics and colors joins forces to smarten up a city apartment designed by Thomas O'Brien of Aero Studios. In the sitting room (opposite), a two-inch band of beige silk borders the creamy-white silk curtains and the simple valance. A similar valance crowns the cotton chintz curtains in the library (above left). The egg-yolk hue of the fabric lends the room a constant look of sunshine. In the bedroom (above right), draperies of olive green cotton velvet are thick enough to block out noise and light from the lively street by night; when they're pulled back during the day, undershades of opaque white muslin provide just the right amount of privacy.

Utterly simple shutters
with inserts of frosty
sandblasted glass
were designer Celeste
Cooper's choice for the
Boston apartment
of a client who admired
a cool modern aesthetic.
In the bedroom, a
serene study of black and
gray, the shutters
eliminate the unattractive
views of alleyways
and air-conditioner units
below while letting in
the light and the views
of treetops above.

I.M. PEI
20th Century Architecture
ISAMU NOGUCHI

the old and the new

Whether in historic homes or cutting-edge modern ones, "architectural" windows ~ those that boast exceptional shape, size, and detailing ~ are beautiful enough to stand on their own.

In older American houses, the overall design of the windows, and the craftsmanship of the mullions and other woodwork, make them exceptional. In the nineteenth century, technological developments made large sheets of glass readily available, and for the first time middle-class homeowners enjoyed big, light-filled windows. Even the simplest houses of the Victorian era featured big sash windows with large single panes. Finer houses, especially those built in the Italianate and Second Empire styles, boasted dazzlingly large windows that sometimes ran the entire height of the wall. Artistic windows with stained glass and leading appeared in houses built around the turn of the century; windows associated with Louis Comfort Tiffany and Frank Lloyd Wright are among the more famous examples.

Anyone fortunate enough to have a house with old windows can accentuate them by leaving them undressed, especially in rooms where privacy is not a consideration. But unadorned antique windows do need great care to look their best. If the window is surrounded by unpainted woodwork, as in many Arts and Crafts houses, the wood should be beautifully finished and polished. Otherwise, the mullions and additional woodwork should be expertly painted. And always, the glass in old windows should be sparkling clean.

Large, airy windows are, of course, an essential part of contemporary buildings. In houses of this style, the metal-frame window is sleek and boldly geometric in shape, and those qualities account for its strong and direct aesthetic appeal. If privacy is a concern, simple architectural treatments such as vertical blinds or aluminum mini blinds are the best solutions. Otherwise, modern windows should be left alone, with light and air as their sole adornments.

Clean-lined windows are the ideal choice for this contemporary Florida living room, which serves as a gallery for modern art. Hal Martin Jacobs, who designed the room, installed big, square, light-filled windows, then pared away all distracting elements to keep the focus on the art collection, including a Louise Nevelson above the fireplace and a Jean Dubuffet between the windows.

Vicente Wolf favors a fresh, modern look for period windows. In the sunroom of a turn-of-the-century house on the eastern end of Long Island, Wolf designed very simple Roman shades of gauzy white cotton. The fabric is fine enough to filter the sunlight and show off the arched details of the original windows when the shades are pulled down.

In a glamorous music room decorated by David Higham and Joanne Jump, ironwork frames inserted in the grand window evoke the design spirit of the 1920s. Filmy white curtains hung inside the arch throw the Deco-style metalwork into relief, and the robust white molding, original to the house, sets off the entire dramatic creation.

Blessed with beautiful proportions and fine lines, the windows in this living room, left completely bare, project an immediate modernity. The strong, graceful arch and dark woodwork surrounding them are so bold and handsome that the best treatment turns out to be none at all.

In a house designed by Washington, D.C., architect Hugh Newell Jacobsen (above), glass doors leading to a porch form a crystalline wall that ushers the woodland greenery into the room. A graphic V-shaped skylight overhead accentuates the sweep of glass doors.

California architect Steven Ehrlich designed the window wall in a beach house in southern California as a giant garage door (opposite). When it rolls up under the ceiling, the room opens up to a deck. And when the door is closed, the Pacific Ocean is the room's dazzling perpetual decoration.

part two

GETTING DOWN TO BASICS

Having a wonderful design in mind for the windows is certainly important in achieving a beautiful and comfortable room. But in order for that exciting vision to become reality, it has to be effectively translated. Not only must the style suit the scheme, but all the other elements must work well, too. The materials have to be well chosen, the details must be carefully thought out, and the entire treatment must be crafted as finely as possible. Practical considerations take on new importance. Hardware, for example, may seem incidental, but if it is not selected for the style, size, and weight of the treatment, the window will not be a great success. As a last concern, the treatment must be carefully installed, sitting comfortably in relation to the woodwork and hanging correctly against the window. The decoration on the facing page by French designer Frédéric Méchiche answered all these requirements beautifully. With artful draping and tucking of a piece of crimson toile and an antique muslin curtain hung high above the frame, he bestowed regal grandeur on a simple casement window. ⊞

inner workings

Turning design needs and wishes into treatments that work ~ and work beautifully ~ requires some careful planning and soul-searching.

People who enjoy the "formalities" of life will probably be comfortable with elaborate designs in which curtains are crowned with valances, trimmed with rich fringe, or hung in multiple layers. But those souls who lead more casual lives will be happier with an understated treatment ~ perhaps venetian blinds, Roman shades, or well-made but simple curtains. For people on the move or in temporary residences, twirling fabric on a decorative pole, nailing a loose ruffle to the window frame, or contriving some other unsewn treatment may be more convenient ~ and more practical ~ than commissioning curtains that will have to come down or be left behind when the lease or job assignment is up.

But even the most beautiful curtain will be unsuccessful if it fails to accommodate the style of the window and the way it opens and closes. Casement windows and some French windows require a treatment that offers no obstruction to the inward or outward swing of the window; sliding windows and doors require designs that won't interfere with the gliding mechanism. The traditional double-hung sash window probably lends itself to the greatest variety of styles, from simple café curtains to frothy balloon shades to full-length, lushly gathered formal curtains.

If curtains are the choice, where on the window or wall will they be hung? Will they fall to the windowsill or to the floor, be crowned with a valance or held open with tiebacks? Will the curtain rod be stationary or adjustable, plain or adorned with fancy finials? If shades are the solution, will they be simple ready-made roller shades or custom-made Roman ones?

On an even more practical note, most window treatments require a commitment to their upkeep, since built-up dust and grime will ruin their look. New York City curtain-maker Henry Norton warns that dry cleaning may wear down certain linings and interlinings. Instead, he recommends "a lot of vacuuming" on a regular basis, which, he says, can actually extend the life of the curtains.

To complement the simple beige curtains in her own dining room, designer Mariette Himes Gomez selected an equally understated valance. Deep enough to give presence to the windows, the valance has an inverted pleat at its center, similar to the kick pleat of a well-tailored woman's skirt.

In an unusual treatment, designers Carlos Aparicio and Jacqueline Coumans used a protruding curved metal rod to hang very full creamy-beige curtains so they stand away from the windows. The undercurtains, falling from a second metal rod, this one attached to the cornice, are mustard linen that appears to glow as the light shines through. The whole design turns the windows into alcoves of golden light.

Louvered shutters instantly create a look of summer. In a design by Stephen Shubel (above), the louvers are part of a single panel hinged on one side of the window. Movable slats allow for the flow of air and the modulation of light while blocking the sun's glare.

Painted Caribbean-blue shutters (right) open inward and have stationary slats.

In a room designed by Rela and Don Gleason, louvered shutters with graceful curved tops accommodate the lunette above the triple-pane casement windows (opposite).

THE ENGLISH ROOM

Swing-arm curtain rods "reminiscent of the high Victorian period in Europe" were Mariette Himes Gomez's tailored treatment for the window wall in a turn-of-the-century Manhattan drawing room (opposite and above). Double panels of gauzy cotton fit neatly over rods attached to the recessed window frames. The designer had the fixtures made in brass, which shines subtly through the soft fabric panels.

Visitors to Ned Marshall's weekend house often admire the window dressing on the French doors (above). The designer's guilty pleasure is in knowing the chic look was achieved by combining couture draperies with chain-store match-stick blinds! The curtains, of classic fern-printed linen, were crafted by Henry Norton, who shares the house with Marshall. They hang from gold-painted rings slipped on a 16-karat white-gold gilded pole that rests at the top of the molding. The blinds are nailed to the French doors.

Decorator Nancy Braithwaite addressed the problem of clearing French doors in a hexagonal sunroom by hanging the rods at the ceiling line (opposite). The billowy full-length organdy curtains are tied to the rods with strips of gold-colored fabric.

The striped sheet turned curtain in a bedroom (opposite) became quite glamorous once it was suspended from a metal shepherd's crook pole. Metal curtain rings like giant hoop earrings add élan, as do the red cord trim and loopy tieback in purple cotton.

A pale blue and white striped sheet was cut and hemmed to a size slightly larger than the window so that it fits loosely (above right). It hangs from ribbon loops slipped over metal drawer pulls that are screwed to the top of the window frame; a decorative gilded rosette holds the panel in a casual swag.

A jaunty curtain concocted from a pink and white striped and flowered sheet dangles from gold curtain rings resting on simple cup hooks (below right).

the material world

A great wealth of materials can be employed in the fabrication of window decorations, so much so that the choices can seem overwhelming. It may be helpful, therefore, to divide the possibilities into two groups, hard and soft.

"Soft" refers to fabric, literally the very fiber of the curtain, the single element that most defines its character and personality. Even without any trimming or fancy hardware to complement it, a silk damask curtain appears formal precisely because of the luxurious material from which it is made. By contrast, a floaty panel of sheer organdy will come across as lighthearted and breezy.

Above all, a fabric should be appropriate for the intended style of the curtain. Lushly gathered floor-to-ceiling draperies call for a fabric that drapes softly and generously ~ a supple cotton or linen, for example ~ rather than a stiff material. The fabric should also suit the style of the room and its architecture. A country cottage is ideal for curtains with playful cotton prints, but it is probably not the right place for taffeta or velvet window panels. Important fabrics look marvelous in a room with grand architecture and fine antiques, but in a room that has neither, an elegant window dressing might look forced or simply out of place.

Washington, D.C., designer David Mitchell always chooses tailored window solutions instead of yards of fabric. Here, a clean-lined heavy cotton Roman shade can be lowered at night for privacy, but during the day it allows for the great streams of light that help give this room its pristine allure.

Intended wear is also a factor in selecting fabric. A woman who invested in fine English chintz curtains twenty years ago is now enjoying them in her fourth home. The survival of curtains from a century or two past in some of the world's great houses is testimony to the amazing sturdiness of fine fabrics.

"Hard" materials tend to be architectural in character, largely because they attach to the window's framework in some fashion. Wooden shutters, one of the oldest kinds of window coverings, look smart, particularly when used in rooms with strong architectural bones and handsome furnishings. Shutters may have movable louvers to control light and air, or they may be solid wooden panels. Plywood is another hard material, often used to form the basis of valances, which crown the top of the window, and lambrequins, which run across the top and down each side of the window, sometimes all the way to the floor, and often covered with fabric. In the most adventurous applications, these wood elements can be painted, or embellished with passementerie or decoupaged paper. Metal can also be made into a valance or sculptural grillwork, usually as a custom commission undertaken by a decorative specialist.

RAISINS

Decorator Carol Glasser opted for an oversize gingham check to team with a large window (opposite) and had the tailored shade made to fit the window's arched recess. The cheery red and white pattern, repeated on the dining chair slipcovers, injects zesty spirit into the Provence-style setting.

Soothing medium-size green and white checks star in the small guest room of Richard Lowell Neas's eighteenth-century French country house (above). To keep the window area unfussy, Neas used a white wood curtain rod and white rings that fade into the cream-painted walls. A canopy of the same woven cotton check attached to the wall turns the small wooden bed into a showpiece.

One-of-a-kind fabric can be created by sewing together pieces of material. Curtains made by top-stitching bands of yellow and white cotton taffeta in graduating widths hang from delicate jute ties threaded through natural wood curtain rings (opposite). Plump jute tassels dangle like playful baubles at each end of the curtain rod.

The only flourish on a view-shielding shade is the wide pieced-fabric border (above). Doubling the curtain's polyester material produced the moiré effect.

Newly installed woodwork by master carpenter Bennett Blackburn forms a fine framework for the leaded-glass restoration windows in the living room of a weekend home (opposite).

Designer Anthony Antine turned the windows in a luxurious bathroom into a splendid asset by brushing the moldings, sills, and mullions with wood graining in a mahogany tone (above). The satiny woodwork is lustrous against the golden gessoed walls and lacquered chinoiserie sink cabinet.

The advantage of shades and blinds is that they lie flat against the window and always maintain a tidy, streamlined appearance. Both are ideal treatments in sparely decorated rooms and in cases where space around the window is at a premium. In a small bathroom (above left), Nancy Braithwaite combined light-controlling venetian blinds with a Roman shade that offers ultimate privacy when lowered.

Wooden venetian blinds on floor-to-ceiling windows emphasizethe minimal style of a contemporary bedroom (above right).

In artist Ken Kelleher's Boston studio (opposite), all plump upholstery and creamy colors, a Roman shade of cotton stripes is the perfect soft touch.

The Boston Globe
Bush expected to lift
sanctions on S.
US says Iraqi report shows
nuclear weapons program
4 companies to pay $69m for Woburn

The imaginative treatment created by Nancy Braithwaite (above) seems straight out of the colonial Caribbean. The shutters consist of panels of grass cloth tied to frames fashioned from two-inch-thick wooden dowels.

Louvered shutters with adjustable slats don't take up any space in the cheek-to-cheek windows in decorator Gregory Cann's cabin bedroom in Maine (right).

A classic European-style shutter made of solid wood panels is an elegant addition to the library of a Parisian home (opposite).

Long and flowing curtains of filmy fabric, generously gathered, always introduce the allure of romance. In a seductively feminine bedroom (above), decorator Pat Sayers hung sheer curtains, then framed them with drawn-back panels and a softly pleated curved valance in cream-colored silk.

Even more voluminous curtains make light of solemn Gothic windows in a room by Beverly Balk (opposite).

fit and trim

Details ~ the finishing touches ~ give window dressing appealing definition and personality. They lure the eye to appreciate the form and line of the treatment, and often of the window itself ~ much the way a necklace enhances the neckline of a beautiful dress.

Finishing touches done in fabric offer as many possibilities as the seamstress's art has discovered. Fabric can be ruched, ruffled, gathered, and pleated into a seemingly endless array of ornaments. It can be cut on the bias to make decorative edging or cut out like cookie dough to provide fanciful shapes for appliqués. Often the fabric used for the curtains provides the makings for the accessories as well, whether it is a pert box-pleated valance or bands for simple tiebacks.

Fine trim provides added luxury and richness. A heavy braided cord with beautiful silk tassels can be the decisive detail that transforms a simple silk curtain into something extraordinary; carefully placed fringe and rosettes emphasize the contours and drape of a beautiful fabric. In all cases, professional curtain trim rather than dressmaker embellishment should be used. It has the correct scale and weight for curtains, and it comes in a wide enough range of sizes to accommodate most windows.

The really big decision with trim ~ with all fabric embellishments ~ is whether to contrast the color of curtains and trim or have them blend. A contrast is exciting when colors and fabrics play off each other, and the effect can wake up the whole room ~ thick white fringe on a red curtain, for example, can't fail to draw attention to the windows.

The question of contrast is true of hardware choices as well. Curtain rods and rings, finials, and holdbacks can all add a burnished gleam. In a contrasting finish, either lighter or darker than the curtain fabric, they can add a bold note ~ dark mahogany rods and rings paired with heavy orange linen curtains, for example.

Finally, there are the unexpected or amusing details ~ trifles or found objects ~ that deliver a punch of their own: gilded finials shaped like arrows, lions' heads, oversize artichokes. Long spears, onetime actors' props, became striking curtain rods when a New Orleans woman hung them in her drawing room. Another homeowner invented glittery fringe by hanging crystal chandelier drops along the edges of cream-colored silk dining room curtains. And in an elegant show house, in which most of the windows displayed "important" tassels and fringe, one decorator drew rave notices when starfish danced at the edges of her curtains.

A simple woven trim, neatly mitered at the sharp corners, draws the eye to the light-hearted shape of this shade. Oversize zigzags can be cut on a ready-made fabric shade or planned as part of a one-of-a-kind machine-stitched design.

Sprightly valances with points accentuate the curtains in the tall bay window of a London town house (above). Sewn of medium-weight taupe and cream striped linen to match the curtains, they sport natural jute banding and playful raffia tassels dangling from each point.

Richmond, Virginia, designers Jane Molster and Deborah Valentine topped off curtains of quilted muslin (opposite) with a tiered effect by tying three different lengths of rabbit-ear ties around the curtain pole, then finishing each with a round wooden ball. The "jester" valances are a bright sally nudging this quiet room to life.

A border of giant lavender blue scallops perks up yards of gathered curtains in a bedroom orchestrated by New York designer Eve Robinson. The color of the scallops appears again in the decorative pillows and loopy bows trimming the bedspread, a repetition of accents that energizes the mostly beige room.

Dressmaker detail enlivens bedroom curtains stitched from plain white sheeting. In this design, easy for the home sewer to master, the three-quarter-inch edging was snipped from a sheet matching the ones on the bed. Cutting the checked sheet in strips produced the jazzy intermittent black and white pattern reminiscent of piano keys.

Ordinary dark taupe linen becomes a chic window dressing with jewels scooped from the sea (left). The row of cockleshells edging the shaped valance and self-fabric tiebacks is actually a tape from a notions shop, stitched on by hand. Marine gems embellish the tieback, and a single starfish anchors the center of the valance.

The gold leaves that shimmer along the top of the sheer pearl-white curtain in Victoria Hagan's living room (opposite above) are really napkin rings, strung along the rod like charms on a bracelet.

A branch masquerading as a curtain rod lifts a ready-made curtain out of its humdrum existence (opposite below) ~ all the better because the odd-shaped branch is longer than the window frame. Twists of rawhide tie the curtain to the branch.

Tassels, cording, and ornamental holdbacks of metal and porcelain are classic adornments from the grand tradition of formal curtain-making. Opposite, clockwise from top left: roping and tassels of silk fringe; a carved wooden tassel; an antique holdback depicting a pastoral scene; a porcelain holdback in pastel colors.

The high-style curtain (right) is the epitome of the curtain-maker's art. Floral striped panels are caught back with decorative cording wound on gilded metal holdbacks. The intricate tassels consist of several large silk-covered baubles dressed in colors blending with the curtain's rich print. The final luxurious touch is the edging of red ball fringe on a cream-colored lining.

Huge rough metal curtain hooks fish for attention ~ and catch it ~ in a breakfast room by Dallas designer Charlotte Comer (above). Banishing pattern entirely from the scheme, Comer arranged dark woods against stark white walls, keeping the windows clean by hanging simple white cotton duck curtains.

In another witty maneuver with hardware, a paddle becomes a curtain rod, casually tied to a billowy sail-like curtain of white cotton (opposite).

The dainty window decorations born in the early nineteenth century are still the height of fashion for neoclassical American houses. For the parlor of his own 1820s home (opposite), designer Michael Stanley devised swags of white muslin and edged them with white fringe to emphasize their cascading form. In the bedroom, he dressed up white muslin curtains by adding a fancy valance with a pert fringe of white wooden toggles (above left).

Even more delicate is the glass bead tassel fringe that designer Richard Keith Langham used as the edging for fine linen curtains on a stair hall window in a Federal farmhouse (above right). The decorative finery was inspired by curtains at nearby Monticello.

In a house with neoclassical overtones, Nancy Braithwaite chose rods with gilded arrow finials for swags of soft cream linen edged with matching cream cord (opposite). Hanging the rods almost at the ceiling made the windows appear nearly half a foot taller.

Braithwaite installed a single heavy linen panel on a sash window in a simply furnished room (left), then revved up the treatment by threading linen self-ties through wooden curtain rings and letting the ties dangle down the top of the panel.

In another breezy treatment (below), designer Carter Kay folded a white linen curtain diagonally to form a pointed valance resembling a giant napkin.

problem-solving

Windows with an offbeat shape or placed awkwardly on a wall or in a room can test the creative ingenuity of even the most experienced designer or curtain-maker. They require special tactics, which often result in ingenious one-of-a-kind dressings that are well worth applying to nonproblem windows as well.

When a window is actually several units, such as a bay window or a window wall with multiple sections, a unified decoration is usually the best approach ~ though the treatment may have to be fabricated and installed in individual sections.

Arched windows, whether they are soaring Palladians or smaller ones crowned with a lunette section, are so beautiful on their own that it is a shame to cover them completely. Treatments that go over such a window's lower section but leave the arch bare are a better solution.

The mechanical requirements of a window may call for special treatments as well. Sliding doors and French doors require designs that allow them to open and close freely ~ especially important when they open onto patios and decks that get frequent use. Hanging the treatment on the wall above the window is a tactic that keeps the treatment out of the way of traffic.

Dormer windows, because they are tucked under the eaves of a house, don't leave much room for a complicated treatment involving a lot of fabric or woodwork. Often, too, these windows are very oddly shaped, thanks to the angles of the house's roof line. Very simple styles such as Roman shades or tailored curtains work best.

Window dressings can also serve as marvelous camouflage for architectural shortcomings. The too-narrow windowsill suddenly looks ample with curtains that extend several inches on each side of the window frame. Floor-length curtains add height to a short window; so does a valance mounted at the top of the frame. And when two windows of different lengths are side by side, combining long curtains with an extended valance can bring harmony and balance to the previously unbalanced window wall.

As a sleek treatment in a library where bookcases butt right up to the window frames, designer Sarah Spongberg installed Roman shades of heavy white cotton.

The custom-made shades are large enough to overlap the window frame on both sides, and long enough to fall gently to the unusually low windowsill.

Designer Vicente Wolf wanted a flexible yet soft-looking way to control the glaring sun in a Long Island house with expansive window walls and a soaring Palladian window (this page and opposite). He solved the problem by making billowy curtains out of yards and yards of gauzy vanilla-colored fine wool and hanging them from a continuous metal rod about six inches above the top of the window frames all the way around the room. The curtains easily slide along the rod at any point to block the sun as the day progresses; at the same time, their gentle color and texture provide a major element of softness in the room.

Treating a large window area as three distinctly separate sections was designer Stephen Shubel's key to solving a potentially difficult design quandary (left). In a bedroom under the eaves, he shaped a trio of cotton canvas shades to accommodate the sloping ceiling.

In another dormer bedroom, architect Alfredo De Vido installed louvered shutters (below). By placing the panels in graduating heights, he introduced an attractive design element, emphasized by the play of light and shade from the sun shining through the wooden slats.

The 1909 house that designer Carolyn Guttilla calls home has second-floor windows with shapely lunettes and handsome wood mullions that she wouldn't dream of covering up. For her bedroom (above left) and the guest room (above right), the designer used diaphanous short curtains with rod pockets and slipped them on rods placed below the lunettes. In the bathroom (opposite), which has complete privacy from the outside, she left the window bare and applied white paint to the woodwork to emphasize the window's pleasing shape against the marine-blue walls.

COUTURE
TIFFANY TASTE
JOHN LORING
Only the Best
Irish houses & castles
AMERICAN WATERCOLORS

Designer Paul Arnold turned a window inconveniently poised over a radiator cover to advantage with a pretty chintz festoon hung from a gracefully arched rod (opposite).

In her diminutive English cottage, designer Nancy Lancaster hung ruffled valances to soften the guest room's dormer windows (above right). In the master bedroom (below right), she gave small casement windows the illusion of grandeur by hanging floor-length curtains on poles extending well beyond the window frame.

What appear to be ceiling-high windows in this sunroom are really walls of screens accented with white woodwork supports. Aiming to turn a porch into a summer living room, designer Carey Reid Kirk clipped lengths of unseamed gauze to wire stretched tautly at the room's corners. When the breeze stirs in this room (many of the fabrics and furnishings are weather-proofed), the giant filmy scarves flutter with all the grace of fine organdy curtains.

The beguiling valances crowning the buttercup-yellow curtains (opposite) appear to be the work of a master curtain-maker. They are in fact a tour de force by decorative painter Robert Jackson, who was commissioned by Sister Parish to create the fantasy valances for her summer living room.

Decorative artist Chuck Fischer crafted a painted wooden valance for his own Manhattan bedroom (above right). An Early American folk art painting inspired the droll set piece; exaggerated swags and tails are decidedly theatrical additions.

More refined but just as fanciful are the trompe l'oeil swags that Fischer painted for designer Libby Cameron's living room (below right). The tin valances sport a star-and-dot motif borrowed from a wallpaper pattern; "underneath," they reveal a faux lining of spring-leaf green.

Artists and Lovers 1900–1930
THE CHATEAUX OF FRANCE

To introduce more texture in her beige-on-beige living room (left), Maryland decorator Sue Burgess turned to an artisan who had experience creating quilted handbags. She backed the woven cotton taffeta curtain fabric with flat felt to give each panel body. Designed without pleats or gathers, the curtains have a simple bias self-band at the top to which thin brass rings are attached.

Quilting can also serve a practical purpose: In her foyer (above), French designer Edith Mézard hung a curtain of heavy quilted cotton ready to be drawn across the doorway when the weather turns cold.

Transporting colors and motifs from Tibet's painted and ornamented monasteries, New York designer Paul Siskin orchestrated a scheme for a summer retreat. Vivid blue paint wakes up the frame of a small window (opposite), which wears a crown of fabric in traditional Tibetan colors. Floor-to-ceiling windows (above left) are dressed with panels called qiqung yola, *crafted of pieced-together sections of black and white cotton and accented with white diamond-shaped appliqués. The center window is topped with bands of yellow, red, and blue, colors that are symbolic of the earth's elements in the Tibetan culture. On the outside, the* qiqung yola *are folded to resemble banners (below left).*

part three

PERSONAL BEST

In the hands of an imaginative decorator, tree branches can be transformed into curtain rods, tiny shells may become the edging on a drapery panel, an Indian sari might be turned into a filmy gold-flecked valance. Some of the most inventive window dressings involve adventurous use of details ~ silver bells instead of fabric trim, embroidered ethnic belts used as tiebacks. Others take their inspiration from couture: A tucked bodice on a vintage satin dress becomes the starting point for a puckered shade. Other expressive designs can be created by exaggerating standard curtain shapes and motifs. The whimsically swagged valances in the room pictured on the facing page are a fantasy interpretation of styles used in English Regency drawing rooms in the last century. They were created by a Connecticut woman who had never tried her hand at design until she plunged into the decoration of her own home, a nineteenth-century Greek revival masterpiece. Her frothy creations are unique and work brilliantly in her airy, high-ceilinged master bedroom. They are proof that window treatments can indeed be highly expressive elements of design. ⊞

minimalism in Milan

The utter simplicity of the white cotton shades covering the windows of Maddalena De Padova's Milan villa testifies to her passion for spare and disciplined design. Others might have romanticized the French windows of the 1930 house with gentle flounces of organdy or white silk Austrian shades, but not De Padova. For her, the completely unadorned whiteness of the tailored fabric shades is both chic and functional.

"In the realm of decoration I am interested only in what is strictly necessary, what is absolutely essential," De Padova says. If the statement rings like a dictum, it reflects the position she has held as a force in contemporary Italian design for more than three decades. In the 1950s, she brought Scandinavian modern design to Italy, then went on to import the work of American innovators George Nelson and Charles Eames. She promoted Italian genius, too, enlisting the skills of native talents such as architect Vico Magistretti. It's no wonder, then, that as the owner of an enormously successful furniture concern, she is often called Milan's high priestess of design.

De Padova's elegant villa is in the heart of Italy's thriving capital of design and finance, but it has the luxuriously secluded feel of a country manor, draped with wisteria vines and set amid the lush greenery of a private garden.

The opaque shades on every window filter and reflect the sun, but they never block it out; here, the light is a powerful and welcome design element, bathing every surface with its glow and filling every space with its brilliance. The pure white shades, white-painted walls, and opalescent wood floors of Danish scrubbed pine all form an enveloping pale background against which the clean-lined Magistretti-designed tables and Shaker rockers stand out. In rooms where extraneous elements have been decisively pared away, the folds of cotton at the window are quiet touches of softness as well, like the white canvas upholstery that appears throughout the villa. Hung high at the ceiling line, each shade is operated by a plain white cord. There are no remote-control devices, no timers to automatically raise and lower the shades according to the sun's course through the sky. The shades are very simple, always the same from room to room. Having discovered a good design, De Padova takes pleasure in repeating it. "Nothing," she says, "counts more for me than simplicity. Along with space, it is one of today's great privileges."

Tailored white cotton shades in De Padova's dining room filter light from the garden courtyard. They are attached to a narrow ceiling cornice, a high placement that allows them to clear the top of the French doors when they are pulled up. Art and Oriental rugs provide the main strokes of color in this spare environment of white and pale wood tones.

The same shade design appears in every room of De Padova's villa, including the second-floor office (left and below) and the master bedroom (opposite). When the shades are lowered, they form a continuum of whiteness with the walls and create a seamless backdrop for her work-table and Shaker rockers.

pouring on the sun screens

Spinning an illusion as dreamlike as any tale in the Arabian classic *The Book of the Thousand and One Nights*, designers DeBare Saunders and Ronald Mayne infused a brand-new winter-getaway condominium in the Bahamas with the romantic aura of a centuries-old Eastern pavilion. The rooms are intentionally evocative rather than based on exact geography. "We didn't want it to be authentic," says Saunders, who envisioned instead "a Westerner's interpretation of the East, almost like something that 1930s Hollywood movie set designers would have done."

Elaborately filigreed window screens hand-carved in India are prominent elements in the decorative fantasy. They extend from floor to ceiling along two walls of the forty-foot-long living room and cover large windows in the other rooms. The designers, inspired by Arabic and East Indian motifs, created their own patterns, dramatically enlarged to stand up to the apartment's airy high-ceilinged spaces. In the living room they used "an overall big leaf incised with smaller flowers, a lot like a lotus leaf." A variation of that pattern, in which leaves appear as a border, was developed for the window screen in the bedrooms. The panels were painted white, connected to one another by piano hinges so they could be folded back, and hung from metal tracks above the windows.

The curved leaves of the screens mirror other sensual shapes in the overall design scheme. From the damask fabrics to the patterns on the wallpaper to the beadwork sewn on the sofa pillows, the surfaces throughout the apartment are rich orchestrations of swirls and arabesques. Playing across them all are the superimposed lotus-leaf shadows projected at the whim of the sun flickering through the screens.

The designers admit that theirs was a decidedly unusual approach for windows that are filled with tropical sun and Caribbean ocean views. "When you own a view like this, you don't always have to see it," reasons Saunders. He believes that the mystery of seeing water and light through the screens is far more tantalizing. At night, when candles glow and light shines in the silk lanterns dangling throughout the apartment, the effect is magical. Says Saunders, "It really is like something from the *Arabian Nights.*"

Set off by a romantic curved arch, the tiled window niche in the living room was once an ordinary bay window; Saunders and Mayne completely transformed it by building a platform and embellishing the entire area with glazed tiles from Turkey.

The filigree effect of the window screens is especially beguiling in the master bedroom (opposite), a cream-on-cream montage of gentle patterns. The room's textural richness is enhanced by two different, though related, screen motifs: a delicate, doily-like pattern on the large window and a giant lotus leaf at the smaller one. Pearls are a luxurious presence, both in the nacreous sheen of the pale walls and the jewel-like edging of the bedspread.

The shutters in the guest room (above) feature grids filled with carved openwork. In a sly reference to the voyage-to-the-East decor, the designers outfitted the room with twin trundle beds, reminiscent of a steamer cabin.

keeping up with history

For period window decorations, America's great-house museums are a wonderful inspiration. By studying how American interior design styles have evolved, homeowners can choose realistic schemes and treatments rather than attempt a slavish interpretation of a particular period. During the past two decades, many of these historic homes have been extensively refurbished, and new decorations have been added based on recently discovered information. A great number of clues have come from close scrutiny of eighteenth- and nineteenth-century paintings of interiors, as well as from Victorian room photographs.

When experts in early American decorative arts at the Morris-Jumel Mansion just north of New York City began a refurbishment program, they were greatly aided by photographs taken in the late nineteenth century. The house was built in 1765 by Roger Morris, a British officer, in what was rural countryside just beyond the city. By 1810 ownership had passed to Stephen Jumel, a wealthy merchant, and his wife, Eliza. Noted in the annals of New York City history for her status as the wealthiest woman of her era and a later, brief marriage to Aaron Burr, Eliza had a taste for elegance. Like other wealthy pacesetters of the freshly minted American republic, she embraced the new neoclassical style of interior decoration. She brought the patterns for her gilded parlor furniture from Paris for her American cabinetmaker to copy and modeled her bedchamber after a painting by the fashionable French artist Jacques-Louis David. When she died in 1865, the rooms she had designed some fifty years earlier were recorded in black and white photographs. Still displayed at the front parlor windows were the daintily swagged Paris-inspired curtains she had hung as a young bride.

Those curtains were copied exactly when the house was restored. They are part of a range of window treatment styles on view in the house, which has been interpreted to show the evolution of American decor from the late Federal period through the late neoclassical era. From the bare-windowed dining room of the 1790s to Eliza's gold-fringed parlor swags of 1815 to the heavy, theatrical swags of the 1830s in the Aaron Burr bedchamber, the windows of the mansion are a marvelous portfolio of historic styles.

Modern replicas of the original neoclassical curtains hung in the front parlor of the Morris-Jumel Mansion sport gold fringe that picks up the gilding on the Empire parlor set custom-made for the room by a New York cabinetmaker around 1815.

Blue-green paint is the main window dressing in the dining room, arranged as it might have been in 1790 (opposite). Wooden interior shutters original to the house were the main form of window cover, providing protection against drafts as well as serving as decoration.

Blue and gold-colored fringe accents the curving swags and cascading tails in Eliza Jumel's bedroom (above), decorated as it would have been in 1820. The curtains, held back with metal rosettes, blend with the fresh robin's-egg blue of the walls, which is authentic to the period.

a tale of two seasons

Designer Paul Siskin didn't start out loving curtains. He had been trained at New York City's Parsons School of Design at a time when the school's curriculum was completely rooted in clean-lined modernism. Pre-Bauhaus design was not acknowledged; ornament was frowned on. And curtains? "You'd probably have been thrown out if you used them, or anything, except maybe Levolors," he jokes. But as a designer, he became intrigued with the elements of traditional decoration. He started to mix classical pieces into the spare settings he created. He added plump upholstery, softening the edges of his minimalist regimen, and tossed in an antique here and there. It wasn't long before he was using curtains "for softening the edges of windows."

Siskin likes window treatments "loose and draped, puddling on the floor," and that is how he hung them for clients in an eastern Long Island house. The homeowners had first enlisted his help in turning the house into a summer getaway. The designer deftly combined the husband's desire for a formal look with the wife's preference for more casual rooms. In the dining room, for example, he added moldings, painted the dado sapphire blue, and installed a fine antique mahogany sideboard to satisfy the formal requirements, then applied imaginative flourishes for the wife's amusement ~ monogrammed burlap slipcovers on the dining room chairs and a boldly striped hemp carpet. But what really shook up the room was the curtains: yards and yards of multicolored striped silk taffeta and as much fun as a circus tent. Unlined, they billow to the floor and put the room at total ease.

Not long after Siskin had moved on to other rooms in the house, deploying tailored Roman shades in the master bedroom and den, the owners asked him to winterize the living room for year-round use. Siskin kept the room's sea grass carpeting and plump upholstery in summery tints of celadon and sky blue, then slipped in a suede wing chair and big leather ottoman, both the color of fudge. Down came the gauze curtains that had dressed the double-height windows and up went flowing curtains of lush sage green cotton velvet. The new materials visually turn up the thermostat of the room on even the coldest day, and both husband and wife couldn't be more satisfied with the room's new casual chic.

Responding to his clients' request for "something about summer" for their weekend house, designer Paul Siskin found silk taffeta with "stripes that look like streamers" for the dining room curtains. He dispensed with lining in order to let the light shine through the fabric and had the curtains made long enough to tumble gracefully to the floor. The brass curtain pole is hung just below the ceiling molding, allowing the French doors to open and close easily.

Cotton velvet curtains of sage green grandly dress the towering bay windows in the living room (above). To be sure that the material would hang smoothly, Siskin had the curtains lined and interlined. They are bordered with natural canvas to tie them to the sea grass rug.

In the master bedroom (opposite), panels behind the bed are wrapped in a taupe and white checked cotton. For a clean line, the designer covered the window with a Roman shade of the same fabric, bringing the shade over the molding to meet the wall panels. The subdued check is an understated foil for the spicy red plaid headboard and bed skirt.

In order to give the den's short, squat windows a taller, more graceful shape, Siskin designed the beige and cotton plaid shades to reach from floor to ceiling. Pulled down, they produce a crisp, sharp look that clicks smartly with the lively mix of plaids on the rug and chairs.

A GLOSSARY OF STYLE

APRON Decorative molding below the windowsill.

AUSTRIAN SHADE A fabric shade that pulls up on vertical cords into swags and appears ruched in soft gathers when lowered.

BALLOON SHADE A fabric shade that pulls up on vertical cords into a puff of material and falls straight when lowered.

BAY WINDOW A window or series of windows with at least three sides that project from the exterior wall of a house.

BISHOP SLEEVE A deeply curved, goblet-like shape created when curtain panels are pulled back, often with special hardware.

BOW WINDOW A semicircular bay window.

BOX PLEAT A tailored, symmetrical pleat made by folding the material to the back on either side of the pleat to create a "box," which is stitched and pressed flat.

BUCKRAM A coarse cotton or linen used as stiffening for valances and tiebacks.

BUMP A cotton interlining used to add body to curtain and drapery panels.

CAFE CURTAINS Short curtains that hang on the lower half of a window and are usually kept closed; the top part of the window is often finished with a valance or another pair of short curtains to create a tiered effect. First used in nineteenth-century Viennese restaurants so patrons could watch passers-by as they dined.

CASING The top hem of a curtain, left open at both ends so a curtain rod can be slipped through. Also called a rod pocket.

CASEMENT WINDOW A hinged window that opens either in or out, like a door, operated by a crank mechanism or by hand.

CLERESTORY A window in a gable or in an outside wall of a room or building that rises above an adjoining roof.

CORNICE A decorative board, often molded or painted, that is attached to the top of a window to create an architectural finish. It can be used with or without a curtain.

DOUBLE-HUNG SASH WINDOW A design invented in seventeenth-century Holland comprising two panels that slide up and down in vertical grooves with the aid of cords or chains concealed in the window jamb.

DORMER WINDOW A window that is set under a sloping roof.

FESTOON Any fabric treatment fixed at the top of the window, including a swag or short dressmaker-style curtain.

FINIAL The fixture at the ends of a curtain rod, either attached to it or added as decoration; originally intended to prevent curtains from sliding off.

FRENCH DOOR A casement window that extends from the ceiling to the floor and features glass panes that run it entire height. Introduced at Versailles in the seventeenth century. Also called French window.

HEADING The top finish of a curtain or drapery panel. It can range from a simple hem that doubles as a rod pocket to more elaborate designs such as pinch pleats, box pleats, or swags.

HOLDBACK A decorative wood, metal, porcelain, or glass ornament attached to the woodwork on each side of the window, used for holding curtains back when they are pulled open.

INTERLINING Soft material sewn between a curtain panel and the lining to add weight to the panel and give it a more substantial hang.

JAMB A side jamb is the vertical molding of a window; the head jamb is the horizontal molding at the top.

LAMBREQUIN A stiff, shaped valance that extends down the sides of a window, sometimes to the floor, and forms a theatrical frame around the windows. Introducted in seventeenth-century France.

MULLION A vertical strip of wood dividing the panes of glass in a window.

PALLADIAN WINDOW A window with three openings, the central one arched and taller and wider than the others. Popularized by the Renaissance Italian architect Andrea Palladio.

PASSEMENTERIE Elaborate, high-quality trim, including braid, cord, fringe, and tassels used as detailing on curtains.

PINCH PLEATS A popular finish for curtain headings consisting of symmetrical, stitched-down triple pleats, separated by flat areas. Also called French pleats.

RETURN The part of a curtain or valance that wraps around the sides of the window.

ROLLER SHADE A simple cylinder containing a spring mechanism, around which the shade coils when raised up by means of a pull cord.

ROMAN SHADE A fabric shade with narrow horizontal rods at the back so that the shade forms a series of softly tailored, nearly flat folds when it is raised.

SPRING-TENSION ROD A rod, usually adjustable, that fits inside the window frame and operates with an internal spring butting up against the window jamb on each side. Often used for café curtains and sheer treatments that hang close to the window panes.

SWAG A piece of fabric elegantly hung between two fixed points at the top of the window and draping down in the center.

TAIL A piece of fabric that cascades from the end of a swag.

TIEBACK A sash, tasseled cord, or separate length of straight, decorated, or shaped fabric that holds back a curtain panel.

UNDERCURTAIN In a treatment incorporating at least two layers, it is the curtain closest to the windows.

VALANCE A finishing touch that runs across the top of the window. It can be either a short drape of fabric or a facing of wood or metal. The English often refer to a fabric valance as a pelmet.

VENETIAN BLIND The classic design of wooden slats joined by tapes and manipulated by cords, which dates at least as far back as ancient Egypt and has been improved upon slightly in modern times by the development of lightweight aluminum and plastic slats.

WINDOW WALL An expanse of glass running from floor to ceiling and wall to wall, sometimes opening by means of sliding metal or wood frames.

DIRECTORY OF DESIGNERS AND ARCHITECTS

Anthony Antine
Antine Associates
Interior Design
New York, New York
Palisades, New Jersey

Carlos Aparicio
Carlos Aparicio Associates
New York, New York

Christian Badin
Christian Badin et
David Hicks
Paris, France

Beverly Balk
Beverly Balk Interiors
Glen Head, New York

Louis Bofferding
Louis Bofferding Antiques
New York, New York

Laura Bohn
Lembo Bohn Design
Associates
New York, New York

Nancy Braithwaite
Nancy Braithwaite
Interiors, Inc.
Atlanta, Georgia

Mario Buatta
Mario Buatta Inc.
New York, New York

Sue Burgess
Burgess Interiors
Chevy Chase, Maryland

Libby Cameron
Libby Cameron Associates
L.L.C.
Larchmont, New York

Gregory D. Cann
Cann + Company
Boston, Massachusetts

Jane Churchill
Jane Churchill Interiors
London, England

Denis Colomb
Denis Colomb Creations
Architecte I.F.I.
Paris, France

Charlotte Comer
Charlotte Comer Interiors
and Collectibles
Dallas, Texas

Celeste Cooper
Repertoire
Boston, Massachusetts

Jacqueline Coumans
Le Décor Français
New York, New York

Maddalena De Padova
è De Padova
Milan, Italy

Alfredo De Vido
Alfredo De Vido Associates
New York, New York

T. Keller Donovan
T. Keller Donovan Inc.
New York, New York

Mary Douglas Drysdale
Drysdale Design
Associates, Inc.
Washington D.C.

Steven Ehrlich
Steven Ehrlich, FAIA
Santa Barbara, California

Chuck Fischer
Chuck Fischer Studio
New York, New York

Carol Glasser
Carol Glasser Interiors
Houston, Texas

Rela and Don Gleason
Summer Hill Ltd.
Redwood City, California

Mariette Himes Gomez
Gomez Associates
New York, New York

Carolyn Guttilla
Carolyn Guttilla/Plaza One
Locust Valley, New York

Kathy Guyton
Kathy Guyton Interiors
Atlanta, Georgia

Albert Hadley
Parish-Hadley Associates, Inc.
New York, New York

Victoria Hagan
Victoria Hagan Interiors
New York, New York

Chuck Hettinger
Chuck Hettinger
Decorative Painting
New York, New York

David Higham
Design Source
Dayton, Ohio

Robert Jackson
New York, New York

Hal Martin Jacobs
The H.M.J. Company
New York, New York

Hugh Newell Jacobsen
Hugh Newell Jacobsen, FAIA
Washington, D.C.

Thomas Jayne
Thomas Jayne Studio
New York, New York

Joanne Jump
Design Resource
Dayton, Ohio

Carter Kay
Carter Kay Interiors
Atlanta, Georgia

Carey Reid Kirk
Carey Reid Kirk Interior
Design and Decoration
Arlington, Virginia

Richard Keith Langham
Richard Keith Langham, Inc.
New York, New York

Joseph Lembo
Lembo Bohn Design
Associates
New York, New York

Ned Marshall
Ned Marshall Inc.
New York, New York

Ronald Mayne
Stingray Hornsby Antiques
and Interior Design
New York, New York
Watertown, Connecticut

MaryAnne McGowan
MaryAnne McGowan Interiors
Greenwich, Connecticut

Frédéric Méchiche
Gallerie Frédéric Méchiche
Paris, France

Edith Mézard
Château de l'Ange
Lumières, France

Lee F. Mindel
Shelton, Mindel & Associates
New York, New York

David Mitchell
David H. Mitchell Interior
Design
Washington, D.C.

Jane Molster
Fine Lines Interiors
Richmond, Virginia

Henry Norton
Van Gregory and Norton
New York, New York

Thomas O'Brien
Aero Studios
New York, New York

Craig Raywood
Craig Raywood Interiors
New York, New York

Eve Robinson
Eve Robinson Associates Inc.
New York, New York

DeBare Saunders
Stingray Hornsby Antiques
and Interior Design
New York, New York
Watertown, Connecticut

Patricia Sayers
Design Resources of
Long Island, Inc.
Huntington, New York

Peter Shelton
Shelton, Mindel & Associates
New York, New York

Stephen Shubel
Sausalito, California

Paul Siskin
Siskin-Valls, Inc.
New York, New York

Sarah Spongberg
Sarah Spongberg Interior
Design
So. Dartmouth, Massachusetts

Michael C. Stanley
Michael C. Stanley Interior
Design
New York, New York

Deborah Valentine
Fine Lines Interiors
Richmond, Virginia

Barbara Wirth
Christian Badin et David Hicks
Paris, France

Vicente Wolf
Vicente Wolf Associates
New York, New York

The room on page 1 was designed by Carey Reid Kirk; page 2, Katie Ridder; page 4, Florence Perchuk; page 7, Ron Shepler and Mark Showell; page 8, Mariette Himes Gomez; page 11, Michel Klein and Joel Fournier; page 13, Bruce Burstert and Robert Raymond Smith; page 142, Sue Burgess.

PHOTOGRAPHY CREDITS

1	Gordon Beall
2	Walter Smalling
4	Jeff McNamara
7	Walter Smalling
8	Michael Mundy
11	Oberto Gili
13	Peter Margonelli
14	Paul Warchol
16	William P. Steele
18–19	Antoine Bootz
20	Christopher Sykes
21	Thibault Jeanson
22	Kari Haavisto
23	Thibault Jeanson
24–25	Scott Frances
26	Antoine Bootz
28–29	Tom McWilliam
30–31	Antoine Bootz
32–33	Tom McWilliam
34	Thibault Jeanson
36–37	Langdon Clay
38–39	Jon Jensen
40	Antoine Bootz
41	Pieter Estersohn
42–43	Thibault Jeanson
44–45	Antoine Bootz
46	David Glomb
48–51	Jeff McNamara
52	Robert Lautman
53	Timothy Street-Porter
54	Jacques Dirand
56	Thibault Jeanson
58–59	Fernando Bengoechea
60	Jeremy Samuelson (top) Dominique Vorillon (bottom)
61	Lizzie Himmel
62–63	Thibault Jeanson
64	Oberto Gili
65	Langdon Clay
66	Scott Frances
67	Antoine Bootz (top) Jesse Gerstein (bottom)
68	Walter Smalling
70	Fran Brennan
71	Jacques Dirand
72–73	Jon Jensen
74	Oberto Gili
75	Antoine Bootz
76	Thibault Jeanson (left) James Merrell (right)
77	Antoine Bootz
78	Langdon Clay (top) Eric Roth (bottom)
79	Gary Deane
80–81	Jeff McNamara
82	Jon Jensen
84	James Merrell
85	Gordon Beall
86	Tom McWilliam
87	Antoine Bootz
88	Jon Jensen
89	Andrew Garn (top) Jon Jensen (bottom)
90	Jacques Dirand (top left) Richard Felber (bottom left)
90	Thibault Jeanson (top right, bottom right)
91	Jacques Dirand
92	Fran Brennan
93	Jeff McNamara
94	Richard Felber
95	Richard Felber (left) Thibault Jeanson (right)
96	Langdon Clay
97	Thibault Jeanson
98	Antoine Bootz
100–101	Lizzie Himmel
102	Jeremy Samuelson
103	Judith Watts
104–105	Lizzie Himmel
106	Michael Skott
107	Michael Dunne
108–109	Gordon Beall
110	Andrew Garn
112	Jeff McNamara
113	Alex McClean (top) Lizzie Himmel (bottom)
114	Gordon Beall
115	Jacques Dirand
116–117	Thibault Jeanson
118	William Waldron
120–122	Antoine Bootz
124	Antoine Bootz
126–127	Antoine Bootz
128–131	Oberto Gili
132	Antoine Bootz
134–137	Antoine Bootz
142	Gordon Beall

ACKNOWLEDGMENTS

The photograph on page 7 was taken at St. Peter's Church Outreach Ministry Designer Showhouse, Rehoboth, Delaware; page 8, Kips Bay Boys and Girls Club Decorator Show House, New York; page 14, American Hospital of Paris French Designer Showhouse, New York; page 16, Kips Bay Boys' Club Decorators Show House, New York; page 28-29, Rogers Memorial Library Designer's Showhouse, South Hampton, New York; page 50, Dayton Philharmonic Women's Association Designers' Showhouse; page 51, Atlanta Symphony Orchestra Decorators' Showhouse, Atlanta, Georgia; pages 58-58, American Hospital of Paris French Designer Showhouse, New York; page 68, National Symphony Showhouse, Washington, D.C.; pages 80, 81, The Castle in Sands Point, produced by Mansions and Millionaires, Sands Point, New York; page 85, Women's Committee of the Richmond Symphony Designer House, Richmond, Virginia; page 86, South Hampton Showhouse, South Hampton, New York; page 92, Historic Preservation Council for Tarrant County, Texas, Designer Showhouse, Fort Worth, Texas; page 97, Atlanta Symphony Orchestra Decorators' Showhouse, Atlanta, Georgia; page 106, Seattle Showhouse of Designers, Architects and Artists to Benefit the Northwest AIDS Foundation, Seattle, Washington; pages 108-109, Southern Maryland Decorators' Showhouse, St. Mary's County, Maryland.